DONALD TRUMP'S ORDER FOR THE RELEASE OF DECLASSIFIED FILES ON JFK, RFK, AND MLK

What Happened in America's Darkest Days

PAUL ZILLMAN

Copyright © 2024 Bay World Publishers

All rights reserved. No part of this publication may be reproduced, distributed, or transmitted in any form or by any means, including photocopying, recording, or other electronic or mechanical methods, without the prior written permission of the publisher, except in the case of brief quotations embodied in critical reviews and certain other noncommercial uses permitted by copyright law. For permission requests, please contact the publisher.

ISBN: 9798309288885

CONTENTS

CONTENTS	4
INTRODUCTION	6
Chapter 1: Dark Days in American History	10
Chapter 2: The Historical Significance of JFK, RFK, and MLK	18
2.1 The Historical Significance of Robert F. Kennedy	25
2.2 The Historical Significance of Martin Luther King Jr.	33
Chapter 3: The JFK Assassination: What Happened and Why It Mattered	40
3.1 The RFK Assassination: A Nation in Mourning Again	47
3.2 The MLK Assassination: Silencing a Voice for Equality	52
Chapter 4: Investigations and Official Findings - J.F. Kennedy	59

4.1 Investigations and Official Findings - R.F. Kennedy 70

4.2 Investigations and Official Findings - Martin Luther King Jr. 74

Chapter 5: Conspiracy Theories and Public Doubts 77

5.2 Conspiracy Theory - Robert F. Kennedy 83

5.3 Conspiracy Theory - Martin Luther King Jr. 91

Chapter 6: The Role of Government Secrecy and Declassified Records 101

Chapter 7: Lessons from History and Their Relevance Today 108

7.1 The Importance of Understanding American History 113

CONCLUSION 116

INTRODUCTION

The assassinations of President John F. Kennedy, Senator Robert F. Kennedy, and Dr. Martin Luther King Jr. remain among the most shocking and defining events in American history. These murders robbed the nation of leaders who had inspired hope, championed progress, and symbolized the potential for a better future. Yet, despite the passage of decades, questions about their deaths linger, clouded by conspiracy theories, incomplete records, and government secrecy.

For many, these assassinations are more than historical footnotes—they are moments etched into the fabric of the country, shaping its political and social evolution. They happened in a period of heightened tension: the Civil Rights Movement was challenging centuries of injustice, the Vietnam War was sowing deep divisions, and the Cold War was casting its shadow across the globe. The deaths of these three figures not only shocked the nation but also left many Americans questioning the very institutions meant to protect democracy and ensure justice.

President John F. Kennedy was a charismatic leader whose vision of a "New Frontier" inspired a generation to believe in the possibility of meaningful change. His assassination in Dallas on November 22, 1963, shook the world. The official explanation pinned the blame on a lone gunman, Lee Harvey Oswald, yet the circumstances surrounding the event sparked endless speculation about larger plots and hidden motives.

Just five years later, Senator Robert F. Kennedy, JFK's younger brother and a rising political force, was gunned down in Los Angeles on June 5, 1968. RFK had been a staunch advocate for social justice and a vocal opponent of the Vietnam War. His death, coming at the height of his presidential campaign, marked another devastating blow to a nation already reeling from division and unrest.

Dr. Martin Luther King Jr., the towering figure of the Civil Rights Movement, was assassinated on April 4, 1968, in

Memphis, Tennessee. Dr. King's message of equality and his insistence on nonviolent resistance had made him a symbol of hope for millions of Americans. His death not only deprived the movement of its most powerful voice but also intensified fears that progress toward racial equality would be stalled or undone.

These three assassinations occurred in an era of political turbulence, but they have reverberated far beyond their time. Each death raised profound questions: Who was really behind these murders? Were they isolated acts of violence, or were they the result of broader conspiracies? What do the lingering doubts say about how Americans view their own government and its accountability?

In 2025, President Donald Trump ordered the declassification of all remaining government records related to these assassinations. This unprecedented move has reignited public interest in understanding what truly happened and why these events continue to capture the imagination of so many. With access to these records, there is a chance to separate fact from fiction and provide a clearer picture of events that have been shrouded in mystery for far too long.

This book is intended to educate, enlighten, and inform. It is not merely an account of the deaths of these three men but an effort to provide context, clarity, and understanding for both students and adults alike. By exploring the events, evidence, and implications of these assassinations, this book seeks to look into long-standing questions that have lingered for so long.

The purpose here is simple: to ensure that the lessons of history are not lost to time, nor distorted by unverified theories. It is a call to examine these events with open minds and a commitment to understanding their significance. The stories of JFK, RFK, and Dr. King are not just chapters in history books—they are reflections of a nation's struggles, its triumphs, and its enduring challenges.

Chapter 1: Dark Days in American History

The 1960s was a decade of hope, change, and revolution. It was also one of violence, heartbreak, and loss. It was a time when America stood at a crossroads, torn between its past and its future. The country was filled with dreams of equality, justice, and progress, but those dreams came at a cost. One by one, four powerful voices were silenced—John F. Kennedy, Malcolm X, Martin Luther King Jr., and Robert F. Kennedy.

They were leaders, visionaries, symbols of hope, each fighting in their own way to make America a more just, fair, and united nation. But instead of seeing their visions come to life, they met the same tragic fate—assassination. Their deaths did not just rob America of great leaders; they shattered the nation's confidence, sending shockwaves around the world. It was as if the very soul of the country had been wounded, and the scars remain to this day.

When John F. Kennedy became president in 1961, he inspired a nation with his words, his youth, and his vision for a better America. He spoke of civil rights, space exploration, and global peace, urging Americans to "ask not what your country can do for you, but what you can do for your country." He made people believe in possibilities, in progress, in a future where America would be a beacon of freedom and innovation.

But on November 22, 1963, in Dallas, Texas, that dream was violently shattered. As Kennedy's motorcade passed through Dealey Plaza, gunshots rang out. In an instant, the young and charismatic president was slumped over, his life stolen in broad daylight. The world watched in horror as the man who had given them hope was gone.

Kennedy's assassination changed everything. America lost its innocence, and trust in the government began to crumble. The Warren Commission quickly concluded that Lee Harvey Oswald acted alone, but many refused to believe it. Questions, suspicions, and conspiracy theories swirled. Had there been a bigger plot? Had powerful forces wanted Kennedy silenced? The uncertainty only deepened the nation's grief.

Beyond America, Kennedy's death was a global tragedy. He had stood as a symbol of modern leadership, a president who challenged the old ways and pushed for new frontiers. His assassination sent a chilling message: even the most powerful, the most loved, could be taken away in an instant.

While Kennedy worked within the system to change America, Malcolm X took a different approach. He was bold, fearless, and unapologetic. He spoke not of peaceful protest, but of self-defense. He urged Black Americans to fight for their rights, to reject white oppression, and to take control of their own destinies. His words were sharp like blades, cutting through the lies of a country that claimed to stand for freedom while keeping millions oppressed.

To some, he was a threat. To others, he was a savior. Malcolm X gave voice to those who had been ignored for centuries, and in doing so, he made enemies—powerful enemies. On February 21, 1965, while speaking in Harlem, Malcolm X was gunned down. His body fell to the ground, but his ideas, his teachings, and his message did not die with him.

His assassination robbed the world of a revolutionary thinker, someone who refused to compromise in the fight for justice. It sent a clear message: speaking the truth could get you killed. Yet, in death, Malcolm X became even more powerful. His words continued to inspire Black leaders, activists, and movements around the world, from the Black Panther Party in the U.S. to anti-colonial struggles in Africa.

While Malcolm X believed in fighting back, Martin Luther King Jr. believed in changing hearts. He led marches, gave speeches, and called for nonviolent resistance. He preached love in the face of hate, unity in the face of division. His "I Have a Dream" speech in 1963 moved millions, painting a vision of a future where Black and white Americans could stand together as equals.

But on April 4, 1968, in Memphis, Tennessee, that dream was cut short. As King stood on the balcony of the Lorraine Motel, a bullet tore through the evening air, striking him down. The leader of the civil rights movement, the man who had given hope to millions, was gone.

The news sent shockwaves across the country. Cities erupted in riots, grief turning into rage. People mourned, but they also demanded justice. King's assassination proved that racism was still alive, that those who fought for equality would always be in danger. It was a national tragedy, but also a turning point.

His death forced America to confront its own failures, leading to the Civil Rights Act of 1968, which aimed to end housing discrimination. The world, too, felt the impact—from apartheid South Africa to human rights struggles in Asia, King's message of nonviolence and justice continued to resonate.

If JFK, Malcolm X, and MLK had represented hope, then Robert F. Kennedy was the last flickering light in the darkness. He was his brother's political heir, a champion for the poor, the oppressed, and the forgotten. He stood against corruption, against war, against racial injustice. In 1968, as he ran for president, he spoke directly to the people, promising to heal the wounds of a divided nation.

But on June 5, 1968, just after winning the California Democratic Primary, RFK was shot in a Los Angeles hotel. He was shaking hands, smiling, celebrating victory, when suddenly—gunfire. He collapsed, blood pooling around him. America watched in horror as yet another Kennedy, yet another symbol of change, was taken away.

With RFK's death, hope faded even further. America was already on edge—Vietnam raged on, civil rights battles continued, and trust in the government was shattered. The 1960s, once a decade of potential and progress, had become a decade of blood and betrayal. The world watched as the land of freedom and democracy struggled to protect its own leaders.

The assassinations of JFK, RFK, MLK, and Malcolm X were not just individual tragedies; they were national wounds that changed the course of history. Each of these men represented a different path to progress, yet all met the same fate—murdered before they could finish their work.

America lost its innocence, its faith in justice, its belief that leaders could make a difference. These assassinations fueled conspiracy theories, deepened racial and political divisions, and left scars that still linger today. They also left behind unfinished business—the fight for civil rights, for truth, for government accountability.

But history shows that even in darkness, light survives. Though these men were killed, their voices still echo. Their words are still read, their speeches still inspire, and their sacrifices continue to push new generations to demand justice, truth, and change.

The 1960s assassinations were dark days in American history, but they were not the end of the story. They were a reminder that the fight for justice is never truly over—and that the most powerful ideas can never be silenced by a bullet.

Chapter 2: The Historical Significance of JFK, RFK, and MLK

It was a brisk January afternoon in 1961 when John F. Kennedy stepped onto the Capitol steps to take the oath of office. The air was electric with anticipation, as if history itself were holding its breath. Americans crowded the National Mall, shivering not just from the cold but from a shared sense of excitement. A young, confident voice pierced the crisp air: "Ask not what your country can do for you—ask what you can do for your country." With those words, Kennedy lit a spark that would ignite an era of ambition, progress, and hope.

But who was this man behind the polished smile and powerful rhetoric? To understand John F. Kennedy's significance, one must step back into the story of a boy from Massachusetts who grew up under the weight of great expectations.

John Fitzgerald Kennedy was born on May 29, 1917, in the suburban town of Brookline, Massachusetts. He came into the world surrounded by privilege. His father, Joseph P. Kennedy Sr., was a savvy businessman and political insider who dreamed of building a dynasty, and his mother, Rose Fitzgerald Kennedy, was a devoted matriarch who instilled discipline and faith in her nine children. John, affectionately called "Jack" by his family, was the second oldest, always in the shadow of his older brother, Joe Jr., who was destined to carry the Kennedy mantle.

Yet Jack wasn't the golden child. He was often sickly, battling ailments from scarlet fever as a child to a bad back and chronic stomach issues as an adult. His health challenges, however, seemed to fuel his determination. Even as a boy, he was fiercely competitive, witty, and curious about the world. These traits would later define his approach to leadership.

Kennedy's education was as ambitious as his family's political aspirations. He attended the finest schools, including Choate, where he earned a reputation as a prankster, and Harvard, where he excelled in international affairs. But it wasn't all smooth sailing. While his older brother was touted as the future president of the United States, Jack was seen as a dreamer—bright but less disciplined. This perception changed during World War II.

In 1941, after graduating from Harvard, Kennedy joined the U.S. Navy. It was during this time that he displayed extraordinary courage. Commanding a patrol torpedo boat, PT-109, in the Pacific, Kennedy's vessel was rammed by a Japanese destroyer, leaving him and his crew stranded in shark-infested waters. Injured but undeterred, Kennedy swam miles to save his men, dragging a badly wounded sailor by the strap of his life jacket. This act of bravery turned him into a war hero and revealed a side of Kennedy that would later captivate the American public: a leader who combined intellect with grit.

After the war, tragedy struck the Kennedy family when Joe Jr. was killed in a plane crash during a military mission. Suddenly, the mantle of family expectations shifted to Jack.

He didn't shy away. Encouraged by his father, he ran for Congress in 1947 and quickly rose through the ranks, winning a seat in the U.S. Senate by 1953. His speeches were filled with optimism and sharp critiques of inequality and complacency. His charm, intelligence, and vision made him a rising star in American politics.

By 1960, Kennedy launched his campaign for the presidency. At just 43 years old, he was young, energetic, and full of ideas. His Catholic faith raised concerns for some voters, but Kennedy addressed these doubts head-on, assuring Americans that his presidency would be guided by the Constitution, not the Vatican. He became the first Catholic president and the youngest man ever elected to the office, defeating the seasoned Vice President Richard Nixon in a close race.

Kennedy's historical significance stems not only from his personal story but also from what he accomplished—or sought to accomplish—during his presidency. His vision of a "New Frontier" inspired Americans to tackle the great challenges of the era, from civil rights to space exploration.

One of Kennedy's most enduring contributions was his commitment to space exploration. In 1961, he boldly declared that America would put a man on the Moon before the decade's end. At a time when the Soviet Union was leading the space race, this goal seemed audacious, even impossible. But Kennedy's words galvanized the nation, spurring innovation and investment in science and technology. By 1969, Neil Armstrong's first steps on the Moon fulfilled Kennedy's dream, symbolizing American ingenuity and determination.

Kennedy's presidency also marked a turning point in the fight for civil rights. Though cautious at first, he eventually became a strong advocate for racial equality. His administration introduced landmark legislation to desegregate public facilities and ensure voting rights for African Americans. Kennedy's televised address on civil rights in 1963 was a watershed moment, as he called for the nation to live up to its ideals of freedom and equality. While much of this work would be completed under

Lyndon B. Johnson after Kennedy's death, it was Kennedy who set the wheels of progress in motion.

Internationally, Kennedy's leadership during the Cuban Missile Crisis stands as a defining moment. In October 1962, the world came dangerously close to nuclear war when the Soviet Union placed missiles in Cuba. Kennedy's calm but firm approach—combining a naval blockade with backchannel diplomacy—helped defuse the crisis without bloodshed. This episode showcased his ability to lead under immense pressure, earning him respect at home and abroad.

Kennedy also championed initiatives like the Peace Corps, which embodied his belief in the power of service. Through the Peace Corps, thousands of Americans volunteered to work in education, agriculture, and health care in developing countries, fostering goodwill and spreading the values of democracy and cooperation.

Despite his many achievements, Kennedy's presidency wasn't without challenges. His domestic agenda, the "New

Frontier," faced resistance in Congress, and his administration struggled to push through some of its most ambitious proposals, including sweeping healthcare reforms. Nevertheless, Kennedy's ability to inspire hope and action remains unparalleled.

Perhaps what makes Kennedy's historical significance so profound is not just his policies but the ideals he represented. He was a leader who believed in the potential of America—not just as a nation but as a concept. He urged Americans to think beyond themselves, to embrace public service, and to strive for excellence in every endeavor. His speeches, filled with eloquence and optimism, continue to resonate, reminding us of the power of leadership rooted in vision and values.

John F. Kennedy's significance lies in his ability to turn ideas into action. He reminded the world that progress is possible when people are united by a shared sense of purpose. His presidency, though brief, left a legacy of inspiration, ambition, and hope—a legacy that continues to shape the American identity.

2.1 **The Historical Significance of Robert F. Kennedy**

On a cold November day in 1925, Robert Francis Kennedy was born in Brookline, Massachusetts, into a family that would become one of America's most influential dynasties. He was the seventh of nine children born to Joseph P. Kennedy Sr. and Rose Fitzgerald Kennedy. His family's wealth and prominence provided a comfortable life, but growing up as the "runt" of the family, Robert, or Bobby as he was affectionately called, often found himself struggling to measure up to his father's high expectations.

As a child, Robert displayed a quiet determination. Though he was overshadowed by his older siblings, particularly his charismatic brothers Joseph Jr. and John, Robert's reserved nature masked a tenacity that would later define his career. Family dinners were lively forums where the Kennedys debated politics and world affairs. These discussions ignited Robert's interest in public service and planted the seeds of the convictions that would shape his life.

Robert's education was marked by change and challenge. He attended several boarding schools in New England before graduating from Milton Academy in 1944. Like his brothers, Robert enlisted in the U.S. Navy during World War II, serving as a seaman apprentice. After the war, he entered Harvard University, where he earned a degree in political science. While he wasn't a standout student, his time at Harvard helped him develop a sense of purpose and resilience. He later attended the University of Virginia School of Law, where he honed his analytical skills and began to form the ideals that would guide his legal and political career.

Robert's early career in public service was heavily influenced by his family's ambitions. In 1952, he managed his brother John's successful Senate campaign in Massachusetts. The experience not only deepened their bond but also revealed Robert's talent for organization and strategy. His success in this role marked the beginning of his rise to prominence in American politics.

From 1957 to 1959, Robert served as the chief counsel for the Senate Select Committee on Improper Activities in Labor and Management. In this role, he gained national attention for his relentless investigations into corruption in organized labor, particularly within the Teamsters Union led by Jimmy Hoffa. His tenacity in these hearings earned him both admirers and detractors, showcasing his commitment to justice even in the face of fierce opposition.

In 1961, when John F. Kennedy became President, Robert was appointed Attorney General. At just 35 years old, he was one of the youngest individuals to ever hold the position. Though his appointment was controversial—critics accused John of nepotism—Robert quickly proved himself to be a capable and fearless leader.

As Attorney General, Robert tackled some of the most pressing issues of the era. He launched an aggressive campaign against organized crime, increasing convictions of Mafia figures by 800%. He also played a pivotal role during the Cuban Missile Crisis, providing crucial counsel to his brother and helping to navigate one of the most dangerous moments in Cold War history.

Robert's commitment to civil rights was another defining aspect of his tenure as Attorney General. He worked tirelessly to enforce desegregation orders and protect the rights of African Americans, often facing resistance from local authorities and federal agencies. He supported the Freedom Riders, dispatched federal marshals to protect civil rights activists, and advocated for landmark legislation to end racial discrimination.

After John F. Kennedy's assassination in 1963, Robert was devastated. The loss of his brother marked a turning point in his life, pushing him to reevaluate his priorities. In 1964, he was elected to the U.S. Senate from New York, where he continued to champion causes close to his heart.

As a senator, Robert focused on issues of poverty, inequality, and social justice. He traveled to impoverished areas across the United States, including the Mississippi Delta and Appalachian communities, to witness the struggles of ordinary Americans firsthand. These visits fueled his passion for addressing systemic inequality and inspired legislative efforts to improve education, housing, and healthcare for the underprivileged.

Robert's opposition to the Vietnam War further solidified his reputation as a voice for the disenfranchised. He criticized the Johnson administration's handling of the war and called for a negotiated settlement, arguing that the conflict was diverting resources and attention from pressing domestic issues. His stance resonated with young voters and anti-war activists, earning him widespread support among those disillusioned with the government.

In 1968, Robert launched his campaign for the Democratic presidential nomination. His message of hope, unity, and social justice struck a chord with a nation grappling with deep divisions. He advocated for policies that addressed the needs of the poor, racial minorities, and working-class Americans. His charisma and compassion made him a symbol of possibility for a better future.

Robert F. Kennedy's historical significance lies in his ability to inspire change and bring attention to the nation's most pressing issues. He was more than a politician; he was a moral leader who challenged Americans to confront injustice and strive for a more equitable society.

One of RFK's most enduring contributions was his role in advancing civil rights. As Attorney General, he enforced desegregation laws and supported the Civil Rights Movement during a time of intense resistance. His decision to send federal marshals to protect Freedom Riders and his public support for racial equality helped to dismantle institutional racism and paved the way for future reforms.

Robert also played a critical role in shifting public attitudes toward poverty and inequality. His visits to marginalized communities were not mere photo opportunities; they were moments of learning and advocacy. By bringing national attention to the struggles of the poor, RFK helped to humanize issues that were often ignored by policymakers. His legislative efforts, such as promoting economic development in underserved areas, demonstrated his commitment to creating opportunities for all Americans.

In foreign policy, RFK's contributions during the Cuban Missile Crisis stand out as an example of measured and effective leadership. His diplomatic skills and ability to find common ground helped to avert a nuclear disaster, showcasing his capacity to navigate complex international challenges.

Robert's opposition to the Vietnam War was another significant aspect of his career. At a time when many politicians avoided criticizing the war, RFK spoke out against the human and economic costs of the conflict. His call for peace and his emphasis on diplomacy reflected his belief in the power of dialogue over violence.

Perhaps RFK's greatest significance lies in the ideals he represented. He believed in the potential of individuals to effect change and the responsibility of leaders to serve the greater good. His speeches often emphasized themes of justice, compassion, and unity, resonating with audiences across generations.

In a speech at the University of Cape Town in 1966, RFK said, "Each time a man stands up for an ideal, or acts to improve the lot of others, or strikes out against injustice, he sends forth a tiny ripple of hope." These words encapsulate his philosophy and his impact on the world.

Robert F. Kennedy's life was tragically cut short in 1968, but his vision for a more just and inclusive society continues to inspire. His ability to connect with people from all walks of life and his commitment to justice make him a figure of enduring significance in American history.

2.2 The Historical Significance of Martin Luther King Jr.

The streets of Montgomery, Alabama, were unusually quiet on December 5, 1955. Buses, typically bustling with passengers, were nearly empty, their seats vacant. Black residents of the city, tired of the humiliation and injustice of segregation, had decided to walk instead of riding. Leading this historic moment was a 26-year-old preacher with a calm but commanding voice—Martin Luther King Jr. Though young and relatively unknown at the time, King's leadership during the Montgomery Bus Boycott marked the beginning of a movement that would transform America forever.

Martin Luther King Jr., often referred to simply as "MLK," was more than a leader; he was a symbol of hope for millions who had suffered under systemic racism. Born Michael King Jr., he grew up in a household rooted in faith and service. His father, Martin Luther King Sr., was a Baptist minister who instilled in him a deep sense of justice and moral responsibility. Young Martin's early experiences with racial discrimination shaped his character and ignited the fire that would drive his life's work.

Raised in Atlanta, King's childhood was marked by encounters with segregation. As a young boy, he developed a close friendship with a white neighbor, but the relationship ended abruptly when the other child's parents forbade their son from playing with him. It was a bitter lesson in the realities of racism, one that left an indelible mark on his heart. Yet, instead of succumbing to hatred, King embraced the teachings of his faith, which called for love and forgiveness even in the face of injustice.

King's academic brilliance became evident early in life. He skipped two grades in high school and enrolled at Morehouse College at just 15 years old. While studying sociology, King grappled with questions of identity, morality, and purpose. Under the mentorship of Dr. Benjamin Mays, a prominent theologian and educator, King began to see the ministry as a powerful platform for social change. By the time he graduated in 1948, King was determined to use his voice to challenge the status quo.

His path to leadership continued with theological studies at Crozer Theological Seminary and a doctoral degree from Boston University. It was during these years that King became deeply influenced by the teachings of Mahatma Gandhi and his philosophy of nonviolent resistance. King believed that nonviolence was not only a tactic but a moral imperative, a way to confront oppression without losing one's humanity.

By 1954, King had assumed the role of pastor at Dexter Avenue Baptist Church in Montgomery. His quiet life as a preacher changed dramatically a year later when Rosa Parks refused to give up her seat on a segregated bus. The subsequent Montgomery Bus Boycott thrust King into the national spotlight. As the leader of the boycott, he demonstrated extraordinary courage and resolve, inspiring thousands to stand together in peaceful protest. The boycott's success marked the beginning of King's rise as a leader of the civil rights movement.

King's historical significance lies not only in the battles he fought but in the principles he upheld. He firmly believed that nonviolence was the most powerful weapon against injustice. His leadership in pivotal campaigns, such as the Birmingham protests and the March on Washington, showcased his ability to unite people from all walks of life. In Birmingham, his strategy of peaceful resistance in the face of brutal police violence revealed the moral bankruptcy of segregation. Images of protesters, including children, being attacked by dogs and fire hoses shocked the nation and galvanized support for civil rights.

Perhaps the most iconic moment of King's career came on August 28, 1963, when he stood before a crowd of over 250,000 people at the Lincoln Memorial and delivered his "I Have a Dream" speech. His words painted a vision of a future where all Americans would be judged not by the color of their skin but by the content of their character. This speech, with its soaring rhetoric and heartfelt conviction, remains one of the defining moments in American history.

King's work extended beyond racial equality. He understood that injustice was interconnected and that the fight for civil rights could not be separated from the fight against poverty and war. In his later years, he turned his attention to economic inequality, advocating for workers' rights and launching the Poor People's Campaign. His opposition to the Vietnam War further demonstrated his commitment to peace and justice on a global scale, even when his stance drew criticism from political allies.

One of King's most significant contributions was his ability to inspire ordinary people to take extraordinary action. He believed that every individual had the power to make a difference, and he worked tirelessly to empower communities to stand up for their rights. His leadership was not just about speeches or marches; it was about building a movement grounded in faith, courage, and a shared vision of a better future.

King's influence extended far beyond his lifetime. His leadership in the civil rights movement led to landmark legislative victories, including the Civil Rights Act of 1964, the Voting Rights Act of 1965, and the Fair Housing Act of 1968. These laws dismantled the legal foundations of segregation and opened the door to greater opportunities for African Americans.

Yet, King's true significance cannot be measured solely by laws or policies. His legacy lies in the values he championed—justice, equality, and the power of love to overcome hate. He challenged a nation to live up to its ideals, to see the humanity in every individual, and to strive for a world where all people are treated with dignity and respect.

In recognition of his contributions, King was awarded the Nobel Peace Prize in 1964, becoming the youngest recipient at the time. His work continues to inspire movements for justice around the world, from the fight against apartheid in South Africa to the ongoing struggle for human rights globally.

Martin Luther King Jr. was a moral compass for a nation. His courage, vision, and commitment to justice remind us that progress is possible, even in the face of overwhelming odds. Today, his dream lives on in the hearts of those who continue to fight for a better, fairer world.

Chapter 3: The JFK Assassination: What Happened and Why It Mattered

On a bright autumn day in Dallas - November 22, 1963 - a moment occurred that would forever change American history. President John F. Kennedy, the vibrant 35th president of the United States, rode through the streets of Dallas in an open-top Lincoln Continental, waving to cheering crowds alongside his wife Jacqueline. The Texas trip had a clear purpose - to smooth over tensions between liberal U.S. Senator Ralph Yarborough and conservative Governor John Connally within the state's Democratic Party. For Kennedy, it also served as an unofficial launch of his 1964 reelection campaign.

The morning began with promise. Air Force One touched down at Dallas Love Field at 11:40 AM. The Kennedys boarded their midnight blue 1961 Lincoln Continental convertible limousine, ready for the 10-mile motorcade route that would take them through the heart of Dallas. Secret Service Agent Bill Greer took the wheel, with Special Agent Roy Kellerman beside him. Governor John Connally and his wife Nellie sat just ahead of the Kennedys. Four Dallas police motorcycle officers flanked the vehicle.

Despite concerns about potential hostile protesters - UN Ambassador Adlai Stevenson had faced an angry crowd in Dallas just a month earlier - the president received a warm welcome from enthusiastic Texans lining the streets. The motorcade wound its way through suburban Dallas and down Main Street before turning right onto Houston Street.

At 12:30 PM, as the limousine entered Dealey Plaza and turned onto Elm Street, passing the Texas School Book Depository, Nellie Connally remarked to President Kennedy that there were certainly people in Dallas who loved and appreciated him, expressing her hope that he no longer doubted it. Her words, filled with warmth, would soon take on a tragic irony.

"No, they sure can't," Kennedy replied. These would be his final words.

Moments later, shots rang out. Most witnesses would later recall hearing three distinct reports. The first shot struck Kennedy in his upper back, exiting through his throat. Though serious, this initial wound would likely have been survivable. The president raised his elbows and clenched his fists in front of his face and neck, then leaned forward and left. Jackie Kennedy, facing him, instinctively reached out to help.

Governor Connally, an experienced hunter who immediately recognized the sound of rifle fire, was also hit. A bullet created an oval-shaped entry wound near his shoulder, destroyed several inches of his fifth rib, and exited below his right nipple, collapsing his lung. The same bullet then entered his arm above the wrist, shattered his radius bone, and finally lodged in his left thigh.

Then came the fatal shot. As the limousine passed the grassy knoll, a bullet struck Kennedy in the head, creating catastrophic damage. Blood and brain matter sprayed outward, reaching as far as the following Secret Service car and motorcycle officers. Secret Service Agent Clint Hill, riding on the running board of the car behind Kennedy's limousine, immediately sprang into action. He jumped onto the street and ran forward, reaching the Lincoln just as the fatal shot struck. Jackie Kennedy, in shock, began climbing onto the trunk of the car - though she would later have no memory of doing so. Agent Hill believed she may have been trying to retrieve a piece of her husband's skull.

The scene in Dealey Plaza erupted into chaos. Some bystanders dropped to the ground, shielding their children. Others, along with police officers, ran up the grassy knoll searching for the shooter. Meanwhile, the presidential limousine raced toward Parkland Memorial Hospital, with Agent Hill clinging to the back of the vehicle.

At 12:38 PM, Kennedy arrived at Parkland's emergency room. Though still breathing, his personal physician, George Burkley, knew immediately that survival was impossible. After futile attempts at cardiac massage, John F. Kennedy, the 35th President of the United States, was pronounced dead at 1:00 PM - just 30 minutes after the shooting.

CBS anchor Walter Cronkite delivered the news to a stunned nation, his voice breaking with emotion. In those pre-internet days, the news spread through television, radio, and word of mouth, creating a shared moment of national trauma that would be seared into the American consciousness.

Meanwhile, a different drama was unfolding in Dallas. Lee Harvey Oswald, a 24-year-old former Marine who had once defected to the Soviet Union, fled the Texas School Book Depository where he worked. He took a bus to his boarding house, retrieved a jacket and revolver, and continued his flight through the city. At 1:12 PM, Dallas police officer J.D. Tippit spotted Oswald walking in the residential neighborhood of Oak Cliff. After a brief exchange of words, Oswald shot Tippit multiple times, including a final shot to his right temple, before calmly walking away.

At 1:36 PM, tired from running, Oswald slipped into the Texas Theatre without paying. Dallas police officers arrested him there after a brief struggle in which he drew his loaded gun. "I'm a patsy," he claimed, denying any involvement in the shootings.

The transition of power occurred swiftly, as required by the Constitution. At 2:38 PM, Lyndon B. Johnson took the oath of office aboard Air Force One, with a still-stunned Jackie Kennedy standing beside him in her blood-stained clothing. Federal judge Sarah Tilghman Hughes administered the oath, marking the first time a woman had performed this solemn duty.

The nation's grief found its public expression in the days that followed. Kennedy's body lay in repose in the East Room of the White House for 24 hours before being moved to the Capitol on a horse-drawn caisson. A quarter-million mourners passed through the rotunda during the 18 hours of lying in state. Even in the Soviet Union, church bells tolled in Kennedy's memory.

But before the nation could fully process its grief, another shocking event occurred. On Sunday, November 24, as millions watched live television coverage of Oswald's transfer from the city jail to the county jail, Dallas nightclub owner Jack Ruby emerged from the crowd of reporters and shot Oswald at point-blank range. Oswald died at Parkland Memorial Hospital - the same facility where doctors had tried to save Kennedy just two days earlier.

Kennedy's funeral service was held on November 25 at St. Matthew's Cathedral, with representatives from over 90 countries in attendance. Though there was no formal eulogy, Auxiliary Bishop Philip M. Hannan read excerpts from Kennedy's speeches and writings. The president was laid to rest at Arlington National Cemetery, where an eternal flame would later mark his grave.

The assassination's impact rippled far beyond that November day. It marked the first of four major assassinations that would rock the United States during the 1960s, followed by Malcolm X in 1965, and Martin Luther King Jr. and Kennedy's brother Robert in 1968. Kennedy was the fourth U.S. president to be assassinated and remains the most recent to have died in office.

3.1 The RFK Assassination: A Nation in Mourning Again

The summer of 1968 brought both triumph and heartbreak to the American political scene. Robert F. Kennedy had just secured victories in two crucial Democratic presidential primaries - California and South Dakota - on June 4th. The Ambassador Hotel in Los Angeles buzzed with excitement as supporters gathered in the Embassy Ballroom to celebrate. None could foresee how quickly joy would turn to anguish.

In the early minutes of June 5th, after addressing his elated supporters, Kennedy made his way through the hotel's kitchen corridor. The choice of this route, meant to lead him to a press conference, would prove fateful. With only minimal security - a former FBI agent and two unofficial bodyguards - Kennedy moved through the crowded space, warmly greeting those he met along the way.

The maître d', Karl Uecker, led Kennedy through the narrow passage, past an ice machine and steam table. When Kennedy paused to greet a young busboy, Juan Romero, the ordinary moment transformed into a nightmare. Sirhan Sirhan, who had been waiting near the ice machine, rushed forward. His .22 caliber Iver Johnson revolver shattered the peace with multiple shots at close range.

Chaos erupted. As Kennedy fell, several people, including writer George Plimpton and former football player Rosey Grier, struggled to subdue the shooter. Five others suffered wounds in the mayhem. Through it all, young

Romero stayed by Kennedy's side, offering comfort and placing a rosary in the wounded senator's hand. Even in his grievously injured state, Kennedy's thoughts turned to the welfare of others.

The news stunned a nation already weary from violence. Television networks scrambled to broadcast the unfolding tragedy, with ABC's coverage taking an especially personal turn - their own associate news director counted among the wounded. At Central Receiving Hospital, doctors fought to stabilize Kennedy before transferring him to Good Samaritan Hospital for surgery.

His pregnant wife Ethel rushed to his side, maintaining a vigil as doctors worked desperately for almost four hours to save him. Despite their efforts, the wound proved fatal - the bullet had struck behind his right ear at point-blank range. Additional shots had hit his armpit, with one bullet lodging in his neck and another exiting through his chest. On June 6th, nearly 25 hours after the shooting, Kennedy's death was announced to a grieving nation.

The killer's motivation stemmed from Middle Eastern politics - Sirhan, a Palestinian, opposed Kennedy's support for Israel during the Six-Day War. His death sentence in 1969 would later be changed to life imprisonment with possible parole, following changes in California law.

A nation's grief poured forth as Kennedy's body traveled from Los Angeles to New York's St. Patrick's Cathedral, where thousands came to pay respects. The funeral train's journey to Washington became a moving memorial, as Americans lined the tracks in silent tribute. At the Lincoln Memorial, the procession paused, allowing residents from a nearby poverty protest camp to join in song. In an unprecedented nighttime ceremony, Robert Kennedy was laid to rest near his brother John at Arlington National Cemetery.

The assassination marked a dark chapter in an already turbulent decade, following the murders of John F. Kennedy, Malcolm X, and Martin Luther King Jr. It spurred change - Congress expanded Secret Service protection to include presidential candidates. Yet the greater loss lay in the unfulfilled promise of Kennedy's campaign.

Born into privilege in Brookline, Massachusetts, Kennedy had grown into a champion for civil rights and social justice. His early career included significant support for Israel, which he viewed as a stabilizing force in the Middle East. As Attorney General during his brother's presidency, he served as a trusted advisor, playing a crucial role in the Cuban Missile Crisis. His brother's assassination in 1963 deeply affected him, yet he pressed on in public service, winning a Senate seat in New York and eventually seeking the presidency.

The 1968 campaign unfolded against a backdrop of social upheaval and anti-war protests. Kennedy entered the race after Eugene McCarthy's strong showing against President Johnson in New Hampshire. When Martin Luther King Jr. was killed, Kennedy's words in Indianapolis helped calm a grieving nation. His California primary victory seemed to signal growing momentum, though he still trailed Hubert Humphrey in delegate counts.

His death altered the course of American politics. Humphrey secured the Democratic nomination amid chaos in Chicago, only to lose narrowly to Richard Nixon in the general election. Beyond political calculations, Kennedy's assassination extinguished a voice that had spoken for unity in a divided nation, for peace in a time of war, and for hope in an era of uncertainty.

3.2 The MLK Assassination: Silencing a Voice for Equality

On a spring evening in Memphis, the world changed forever. At 6:01 p.m. on April 4, 1968, a single shot rang out at the Lorraine Motel, forever silencing one of America's most powerful voices for civil rights and human dignity. Dr. Martin Luther King Jr., who had faced death threats since the 1950s, fell on the motel's balcony — a moment that would send shockwaves across a nation already grappling with profound social change.

The story begins with purpose. King had traveled to Memphis to support striking African-American sanitation workers, men who endured unfair wages and deplorable working conditions under Mayor Henry Loeb's administration. These workers, who received significantly lower pay than their white counterparts, worked without proper uniforms or restrooms, lacking even basic dignity in their labor. The February 1968 deaths of two workers in a garbage-compacting truck had transformed simmering frustration into determined action.

Just one day before his death, King delivered what would become his final speech at the Mason Temple. His words that evening seemed touched by prophecy. He spoke of an earlier brush with death – a 1958 stabbing that had brought him so close to the end that doctors warned even a sneeze might have killed him. With passionate eloquence, he wove this personal story into the broader tapestry of the civil rights movement, recalling sit-ins, freedom rides, and marches that had slowly bent the arc of history toward justice.

In what would become his final moments, King stood on the balcony of Room 306 – a room he had stayed in so often with his colleague Rev. Ralph Abernathy that it was known as the "King-Abernathy Suite."

The fatal shot struck King in the face at 6:01 p.m., fired from a Remington Model 760 rifle. The bullet's path was devastating, breaking his jaw and vertebrae, cutting through vital arteries before coming to rest in his shoulder. The force was so great it tore away his necktie. As colleagues rushed to his aid, the shooter fled from a nearby rooming house, leaving behind a package containing a rifle and binoculars marked with fingerprints.

The response to King's assassination revealed the deep fissures in American society. While some called for peaceful remembrance in keeping with his philosophy, others saw his death as the end of nonviolent resistance. Stokely Carmichael expressed his anger by stating that White America was responsible for Dr. King's death the previous night. He emphasized that there was no longer a need for intellectual discussions, as Black people now understood that they had to arm themselves.

Despite calls for calm from movement leaders, more than 100 cities erupted in riots. Yet in Memphis itself, the sanitation workers' strike that had brought King to the city was quickly settled in the workers' favor – a bittersweet victory sealed in blood.

The nation's leaders responded with varying degrees of grace and understanding. President Johnson canceled his planned Vietnam War meeting, declared a national day of mourning, and personally called Coretta Scott King. Robert F. Kennedy, campaigning in Indianapolis, delivered an impromptu speech that helped prevent riots in that city, drawing on his own experience of losing a brother to violence.

On April 8, Coretta Scott King led 40,000 people in a silent march through Memphis, a powerful demonstration of dignity in grief. The next day, Atlanta hosted funeral services that drew more than 100,000 mourners who followed King's body from Ebenezer Baptist Church to Morehouse College. At his widow's request, his final sermon played during the service – words in which he had asked to be remembered not for his awards and honors, but for his efforts to feed the hungry, clothe the naked, stand against war, and serve humanity.

James Earl Ray, the man identified as King's assassin, was captured two months later at London's Heathrow Airport. He pleaded guilty to first-degree murder in March 1969 and received a 99-year sentence, though he later recanted his confession. The King family would later support claims of a broader conspiracy, winning a symbolic civil lawsuit in 1999 against Loyd Jowers and unnamed others – though the Justice Department later disputed these findings.

The assassination of Dr. King marked the third of four major political murders that scarred America in the 1960s, following President Kennedy and Malcolm X, and preceding Robert Kennedy's death just two months later. Each death diminished the nation, but King's loss held special significance. He had prophetically prepared both himself and his followers for this possibility, teaching that murder could not stop the struggle for equal rights.

King's death came as he was expanding his mission beyond civil rights to address poverty and oppose the Vietnam War. His last campaign in Memphis embodied this broader vision, fighting for the dignity of workers who simply wanted fair treatment and basic human respect. The shot that took his life also robbed America of a voice that might have helped guide the nation through the turbulent years ahead.

In death, as in life, King forced America to confront its contradictions. While many whites expressed genuine grief, others responded with shocking callousness. The disparate reactions highlighted the deep racial divisions King had worked to heal. His assassination became a turning point that simultaneously advanced his cause through national shock and remorse while also fragmenting the civil rights movement he had helped unite.

The true measure of this loss extends far beyond that April evening in Memphis. It lives in the dreams deferred, the words never spoken, the bridges never built. Yet King's final speech seems to answer even this tragedy: "I've been to the mountaintop... I've seen the promised land. I may not get there with you. But I want you to know tonight, that we, as a people, will get to the promised land!"

Chapter 4: Investigations and Official Findings - J.F. Kennedy

The assassination of President John F. Kennedy on November 22, 1963, set in motion a series of investigations unprecedented in American history, each seeking to uncover the truth behind this watershed moment. From the initial police work in Dallas to decades of federal investigations, the quest for answers would reveal both facts and controversies that continue to resonate today.

Within hours of Kennedy's death, the Dallas Police Department began their investigation by interrogating Lee Harvey Oswald about both Kennedy's assassination and the killing of Officer J.D. Tippit. Captain J. W. Fritz of the Homicide and Robbery Bureau led approximately 12 hours of intermittent questioning between 2:30 p.m. on November 22 and 11 a.m. on November 24. The interrogation process immediately showed concerning flaws - Fritz kept only basic notes and wrote his report days later from memory. No stenographic or tape recordings were made, despite the presence of FBI and Secret Service representatives who occasionally participated in the questioning.

The Dallas Police conducted paraffin tests on Oswald's hands and right cheek to determine if he had recently fired a weapon. While the results were positive for his hands and negative for his cheek, these tests were known to be unreliable, and the Warren Commission would later dismiss them. The police department's handling of the case raised serious concerns, particularly their decision to force Oswald to participate in a press conference after midnight on November 23 and their numerous unauthorized leaks to the media. These actions so angered President Johnson that he instructed the FBI to tell them to stop discussing the assassination publicly.

The FBI launched its own investigation immediately after the shooting, using a federal statute about assaulting federal officers as their jurisdiction. FBI Director J. Edgar

Hoover moved with remarkable - perhaps suspicious - speed, sending President Johnson a preliminary report within 24 hours that identified Oswald as the sole perpetrator. After Jack Ruby killed Oswald, Johnson, having lost faith in Texas authorities, directed the FBI to conduct a complete investigation.

The FBI's work was extensive - 169 agents conducted over 25,000 interviews and produced more than 2,300 reports. Their December 9, 1963 report to the Warren Commission concluded that three bullets had been fired: one striking Kennedy's upper back, another hitting Connally, and the fatal shot to Kennedy's head. While some praised the FBI's thoroughness, the House Select Committee on Assassinations would later criticize their investigation of pro- and anti-Castro Cubans and potential connections to Oswald or Ruby as insufficient. They also noted Hoover's apparent determination to establish Oswald as the lone assassin within the first 24 hours.

President Johnson established the Warren Commission on November 29, selecting Supreme Court Chief Justice Earl

Warren to chair the investigation. Their 888-page final report, released in September 1964, concluded that Oswald acted alone in killing Kennedy and wounding Connally, and that Ruby acted independently in killing Oswald. The commission noted Oswald's Marxism, anti-authoritarianism, violent tendencies, failure to form relationships, and desire for historical significance, though they made no definitive conclusions about his motives.

One of the commission's most crucial - and controversial - findings emerged when staffers examined the Zapruder film and realized the FBI's shooting theory was impossible. The reaction times of Kennedy and Connally were too close together to have been caused by separate bullets, given Oswald's 2.3-second reload time. This led to the "single-bullet theory" - that one bullet caused both men's non-fatal wounds. Commission staffer Arlen Specter conducted a reenactment in Dealey Plaza that showed the bullet's path aligned with both men's injuries.

However, three commission members - Representative Hale Boggs and Senators John Cooper and Richard Russell

- privately considered this theory "improbable," though their doubts weren't mentioned in the final report. Critics dubbed it the "magic bullet theory," partly because the bullet appeared surprisingly intact. However, HSCA pathologist Michael Baden noted the bullet was fundamentally deformed despite its lack of fragmentation. In 2023, new information emerged when Secret Service Agent Paul Landis told The New York Times that he had retrieved this bullet from behind Kennedy's seat at Parkland Hospital and placed it on Kennedy's stretcher, suggesting it had dislodged from a shallow back wound.

The Warren Commission generated unprecedented documentation - 27 published volumes plus hundreds of thousands of pages of investigative materials. While some praised its thoroughness, others criticized its reliance on the FBI and CIA to investigate themselves. A 2014 report by CIA Chief Historian David Robarge revealed that then-CIA director John A. McCone participated in a "benign cover-up" by withholding information from the commission.

The only criminal trial related to the assassination began in 1967 when New Orleans District Attorney Jim Garrison charged businessman Clay Shaw with conspiracy. Shaw, a respected figure who had helped preserve the French Quarter, seemed an unlikely suspect. Both he and another alleged conspirator, David Ferrie, were part of New Orleans' gay community. Ferrie died, possibly by suicide, shortly after the investigation became public. During the 34-day trial in 1969, Garrison played the Zapruder film and argued that Kennedy's backward head movement after the fatal shot indicated a shooter on the grassy knoll.

The jury quickly acquitted Shaw, though controversy surrounded the verdict and trial. While conspiracy theorist Mark Lane claimed some jurors believed Shaw was involved but lacked sufficient evidence to convict, playwright James Kirkwood disputed these assertions. The trial is now widely considered a "travesty of justice," with some viewing it as motivated by homophobia. Later revelations showed Shaw had been a part-time CIA contact, though this was true of approximately 150,000 Americans at the time.

In 1968, Attorney General Ramsey Clark convened a panel of four medical experts to examine Kennedy's autopsy photographs and X-rays, which most Warren Commission members hadn't viewed. The panel supported the commission's findings that Kennedy was struck by two bullets from behind. The 1975 Rockefeller Commission, established by President Gerald Ford, also examined these materials and agreed with this conclusion. They addressed the backward motion of Kennedy's head seen in the Zapruder film, attributing it to a "seizure-like neuromuscular reaction" rather than evidence of a frontal shot.

The Church Committee, formed in 1975 following Watergate and revelations of CIA misconduct, found no evidence of a CIA or FBI conspiracy but criticized both agencies for withholding information from the Warren Commission. Significantly, they revealed that the CIA had conspired with the Mafia in multiple failed attempts to assassinate Cuban leader Fidel Castro, information that might have significantly affected the original investigation.

The House Select Committee on Assassinations (HSCA) conducted its investigation from 1976 to 1978, concluding that Kennedy was "likely assassinated as a result of a conspiracy." They suggested a "high probability" that a fourth shot was fired from the grassy knoll, though they believed this shot missed. However, their conspiracy conclusion primarily rested on acoustic analysis of a police Dictabelt recording that was later discredited by both the FBI's Technical Services Division and a National Academy of Sciences Committee.

The HSCA found previous investigations into Oswald's responsibility "thorough and reliable" but criticized their inadequate investigation of possible conspiracy. They noted that federal agencies performed with "varying degrees of competency," with the FBI and CIA failing to share all relevant information with other agencies and the Warren Commission. The Secret Service was criticized for inadequate analysis of pre-assassination information and insufficient presidential protection.

The release of Oliver Stone's film "JFK" in 1991 renewed public interest and led to the JFK Records Act, which mandated the release of all assassination-related documents within 25 years. The resulting Assassination Records Review Board gathered and unsealed about 60,000 documents containing over 4 million pages between 1994 and 1998. A 1998 staff report raised questions about the authenticity of Kennedy's brain photographs in official records, noting they showed less damage than described by witnesses at both Parkland Hospital and the autopsy. The board emphasized the challenges of witness testimony, urging consideration of all evidence rather than relying on single statements.

The autopsy itself, conducted at Bethesda Naval Hospital, has been widely criticized as the "most botched" segment of the government's investigation. The HSCA forensic pathology panel identified "extensive failings," including insufficient photography, failure to determine exact bullet entry and exit points, incomplete dissection of the back and neck, and inadequate analysis of gunshot angles relative to body position. The selection of Commander

James Humes, who had minimal forensic pathology training, to lead the autopsy was particularly criticized. New York City Chief Medical Examiner Milton Helpern compared the situation to sending a seven-year-old boy with only three violin lessons to perform a Tchaikovsky symphony with the New York Philharmonic, highlighting the unrealistic expectations involved.

The mysterious disappearance of Kennedy's preserved brain three years after the autopsy when the Kennedy family transferred materials to the National Archives added another layer of controversy. While conspiracy theorists suggested the brain might have shown evidence of a frontal shot, the HSCA concluded that an assistant to Attorney General Robert F. Kennedy likely removed the materials at Kennedy's direction, either destroying them or making them inaccessible to prevent misuse or to hide the president's chronic health issues.

The release of assassination records has continued into recent years. President Donald Trump initially promised to release all documents but later blocked some records until

October 2021. President Joe Biden further delayed the release, citing the COVID-19 pandemic, before releasing 13,173 unredacted documents in 2022. A second group of files was unsealed in June 2023, bringing the total to 99 percent of all documents made public.

These investigations represent an unprecedented effort to uncover the truth behind one of America's most traumatic moments. While they answered many questions, they also revealed institutional failures, conflicting evidence, and the challenges of establishing definitive truth in the face of complex historical events. The intensity and scope of these investigations, spanning multiple decades and generating millions of pages of documents, reflect both the magnitude of the tragedy and its enduring impact on American society. The fact that discussions and document releases continue six decades later demonstrates how deeply this event has marked American history and consciousness.

4.1 Investigations and Official Findings - R.F. Kennedy

Sirhan Sirhan, the man convicted of assassinating Senator Robert F. Kennedy, was born on March 19, 1944, in Jerusalem, Palestine, into an Arab Christian family. At the age of four, he and his father barely survived a bomb explosion during the 1948 Palestine War. According to author Mel Ayton, this experience deeply affected Sirhan's psychological state.

During his childhood, he witnessed multiple violent events, including his father's physical abuse and the death of his older brother, who was struck by a military truck while the driver attempted to avoid sniper fire. In late 1956, Sirhan's family moved to the United States, a transition he resented. He later expressed that he felt the U.S. supported Israel, and since Israel was an enemy of his people, he viewed America in the same light.

Despite his early struggles, Sirhan did well in school, earning above-average grades and joining an officer candidate program. However, his late teenage years were marked by personal hardships. His father abandoned the family, his sister passed away, two of his brothers were arrested, and he was eventually expelled from Pasadena City College. He developed strong anti-Zionist and pro-Palestinian beliefs, which later played a role in his hatred toward Robert F. Kennedy.

In 1966, Sirhan pursued a career as a jockey, but after falling from a horse, he sustained minor injuries. A friend later recalled that, after this accident, Sirhan became impatient, nervous, and emotionally unstable. During an investigation, authorities found a diary in his home, where he had written on May 18, 1968, that "Robert Kennedy must be assassinated" and that his determination to kill RFK had become an unshakable obsession.

Since Sirhan was not a U.S. citizen, California law prohibited him from purchasing firearms. By possessing the gun used in the assassination, he violated three state laws. Some researchers, including Loren Coleman, have suggested that the date of Kennedy's assassination was symbolic, as it marked the first anniversary of the Six-Day War between Israel and its Arab neighbors.

Upon Sirhan's arrest, police found a newspaper clipping in his pocket, discussing Kennedy's support for Israel. Sirhan later admitted that his hatred for RFK began after learning about his pro-Israel stance. In April 1969, Sirhan was convicted of Kennedy's murder and sentenced to death. However, in 1972, his sentence was reduced to life in prison after the California Supreme Court ruled that all death sentences issued before 1972 were unconstitutional.

In 1975, officials set a parole date for Sirhan in 1984, but this was later revoked in 1982 after he allegedly made threats while in prison. In a 1989 interview with David Frost, Sirhan stated that his only connection to Kennedy was Kennedy's support for Israel and his decision to send bombers to Israel, which Sirhan believed would harm the Palestinian people.

Some researchers have described Sirhan as a withdrawn fanatic with identity struggles, but historian James W. Clarke argued that his motives were primarily political, rather than personal or psychological. Throughout his trial, Sirhan's lawyers attempted to argue diminished responsibility, but he repeatedly tried to plead guilty, admitting that he had killed Kennedy with "20 years of malice aforethought."

For decades, questions have been raised about whether Sirhan acted alone. In 2012, his attorneys William F. Pepper and Laurie Dusek filed a petition in Los Angeles District Court, claiming that a second gunman fired the fatal shots that killed RFK. This was part of a series of federal petitions under habeas corpus, which had begun in 2010.

During Sirhan's 2016 parole hearing, Paul Schrade, one of the victims wounded in the shooting, publicly stated that Sirhan did not fire the fatal shots. Schrade accused the Los Angeles Police Department (LAPD) of tampering with ballistic evidence, destroying key findings, and covering up proof that a second shooter had killed Robert Kennedy.

In August 2021, a California parole panel recommended Sirhan's release. The decision divided Kennedy's family. Two of RFK's children, Robert Jr. and Douglas Kennedy, supported parole, believing that Sirhan had served his time. However, six other Kennedy siblings strongly opposed his release, stating that justice had not yet been fully served.

In January 2022, California Governor Gavin Newsom denied Sirhan's parole, stating that Sirhan had not demonstrated full accountability for his actions, making his release a risk to public safety.

4.2 Investigations and Official Findings - Martin Luther King Jr.

Following Dr. Martin Luther King Jr.'s assassination, the Federal Bureau of Investigation (FBI) was assigned to lead the investigation. J. Edgar Hoover, the FBI director who had previously worked to discredit King, assured President Lyndon B. Johnson that his agency would identify those responsible.

The FBI gathered fingerprints and ballistic evidence from the bathroom where the gunfire originated. They recovered a Remington Gamemaster rifle, which had fired at least one shot, and traced the fingerprints to James Earl Ray, an escaped convict. After two months on the run, Ray was captured at London's Heathrow Airport, attempting to flee under a false Canadian passport.

Ray later confessed to the crime, pleading guilty on March 10, 1969, to avoid the death penalty. He was sentenced to 99 years in prison but later recanted his confession, claiming he was manipulated into pleading guilty. Over the years, he insisted that a mysterious figure named "Raoul" was involved in a larger conspiracy.

Despite the FBI's conclusion that Ray acted alone, many documents remain classified until 2027, fueling ongoing doubts and calls for full disclosure of all government records related to King's assassination.

Chapter 5: Conspiracy Theories and Public Doubts

Conspiracy theories have always fascinated the public, feeding on uncertainty and distrust. Few historical events have generated as many theories and persistent doubts as the assassination of President John F. Kennedy on November 22, 1963. The shock of that day left Americans grasping for answers, and despite official investigations, the belief that Kennedy's death was part of a larger plot remains deeply embedded in public consciousness. The official narrative, as presented by the Warren Commission in 1964, concluded that a lone gunman, Lee Harvey Oswald, fired the fatal shots from the sixth floor of the Texas School Book Depository. Yet, from the moment the shots rang out in Dealey Plaza, skepticism took root. Witnesses described hearing gunfire from multiple directions, and the dramatic murder of Oswald by nightclub owner Jack Ruby just two days later only deepened suspicions. How could a lone assassin execute such a crime, and why would a seemingly ordinary man like Ruby silence him before he could stand trial? These questions ignited theories that have refused to fade.

The idea that Oswald was not acting alone but was instead part of a broader conspiracy gained momentum almost immediately. Theories emerged, pointing fingers at different power structures, including the CIA, the Mafia, the KGB, Cuban leader Fidel Castro, and even Vice President Lyndon B. Johnson. Investigative journalist Vincent Bugliosi estimated that over 40 groups, 80 assassins, and more than 200 individuals have been implicated in various theories. This overwhelming number reflects the sheer extent of public doubt, as people struggle to accept that such a significant event could have been carried out by one man acting in isolation. The doubts were further reinforced by inconsistencies and contradictions in the official investigations. The Warren Commission's findings were widely criticized, with many believing that evidence had been manipulated or suppressed. Critics argued that the Commission relied too heavily on reports from the FBI and CIA, both of which had their own interests at stake.

In 1979, the United States House Select Committee on Assassinations (HSCA) reopened the case and reached a startling conclusion: Kennedy was likely assassinated as part of a conspiracy. The Committee found that at least four shots had been fired, rather than the three claimed by the Warren Commission, and that two gunmen had likely been involved. The findings intensified public skepticism, suggesting that the initial investigation had failed to uncover the full truth. However, despite acknowledging the probability of a conspiracy, the HSCA could not definitively identify the individuals or groups responsible. This vague conclusion only fueled more speculation, leaving the door open for decades of continued debate.

Public opinion polls have consistently shown that most Americans believe Kennedy's assassination involved more than just Oswald. In the immediate aftermath of the shooting, 62 percent of those surveyed believed others had been involved. By the late 1970s and early 1980s, this number had risen to over 80 percent, demonstrating the widespread rejection of the lone-gunman theory. Even in recent years, surveys indicate that a majority of Americans still suspect a cover-up. This persistent belief is not without reason. The delayed release of government documents has reinforced suspicions that the full truth remains hidden. Under the President John F. Kennedy Assassination Records Collection Act of 1992, most documents related to the assassination were scheduled for release by 2017. However, subsequent delays by Presidents Donald Trump and Joe Biden pushed back the release, citing concerns over national security. While thousands of records have now been declassified, some files remain undisclosed, leaving room for continued speculation.

Among the most enduring conspiracy theories is the claim that there was a second shooter on the grassy knoll, a small hill in Dealey Plaza. Witnesses at the scene reported hearing gunfire from this direction, and the famous Zapruder film, which captured the assassination in detail, shows Kennedy's head snapping backward, which many interpret as evidence of a shot from the front. This contradicts the official account that all shots came from behind. The single-bullet theory, which suggests that one bullet passed through both Kennedy and Texas Governor John Connally, has also been heavily disputed. Critics argue that the trajectory described in the Warren Commission's report is implausible and that separate bullets must have struck the two men, further implying the presence of multiple shooters.

Other theories point to potential motives for eliminating Kennedy. Some suggest that the CIA orchestrated the assassination due to Kennedy's reported dissatisfaction with the agency following the failed Bay of Pigs invasion. Others argue that the Mafia played a role, seeking revenge for his administration's crackdown on organized crime. The possibility of foreign involvement has also been widely debated, with theories suggesting that the Soviet Union or Cuba had reason to eliminate Kennedy due to Cold War tensions. These theories persist because each has circumstantial evidence that, while not definitive, raises enough questions to prevent the official story from being universally accepted.

Further complicating matters are allegations that key witnesses were silenced. Many individuals connected to the assassination died under unusual circumstances, leading to speculation that they were eliminated to prevent them from revealing the truth. Journalist Dorothy Kilgallen, who had conducted an exclusive interview with Jack Ruby, was found dead under mysterious circumstances. Other deaths, including those of eyewitnesses, law enforcement officials, and even suspects, have been labeled suspicious by researchers who believe they form a pattern too significant to ignore.

The release of declassified documents has provided some insight into the government's handling of the case, but rather than putting conspiracy theories to rest, they have often raised more questions. For instance, a CIA memo from 1963 revealed that intelligence officials had intercepted calls made by someone impersonating Oswald in Mexico City just weeks before the assassination. This has led to speculation that Oswald was being framed or manipulated by forces beyond his control. Similarly, FBI

Director J. Edgar Hoover's internal memo, stating that the public needed to be convinced that Oswald was the real assassin, has been cited as evidence of a coordinated effort to control the narrative.

Despite the passage of time, Kennedy's assassination remains one of the most debated topics in American history. Theories continue to evolve as new evidence surfaces, and the belief in a conspiracy has not diminished. Whether it was a lone gunman, a carefully orchestrated plot, or a combination of both, the doubts surrounding Kennedy's death reflect a broader distrust in official narratives. The assassination was more than just the tragic loss of a president—it became a symbol of deeper uncertainties about power, secrecy, and the limits of what the public is allowed to know. Until every question is answered, the theories will persist, and the search for the truth will continue.

5.2 Conspiracy Theory - Robert F. Kennedy

Conspiracy theories have always captivated public attention, particularly when they involve high-profile assassinations. The killing of Robert F. Kennedy on June 5, 1968, in Los Angeles, California, is no exception. Much like the assassination of his brother, President John F. Kennedy, Robert Kennedy's death has been the subject of intense debate and speculation. Officially, Sirhan Sirhan was convicted of the murder and remains in prison for the crime. However, countless theories suggest that the true circumstances surrounding his assassination were far more complicated. The idea that Sirhan did not act alone, that evidence was mishandled, and that powerful forces may have been involved continues to fuel public skepticism.

Kennedy had just won the California primary and was celebrating at the Ambassador Hotel when he was shot. His death the following day at Good Samaritan Hospital shocked the nation. While Sirhan Sirhan was quickly arrested and convicted, many have questioned whether he was the only gunman. Witness accounts, forensic inconsistencies, and audio evidence have led some to believe that a second shooter was involved. This theory largely stems from the fact that Kennedy's fatal wound was located behind his right ear, fired at close range, even though Sirhan was seen standing in front of him. Los Angeles County's Chief Medical Examiner-Coroner, Thomas Noguchi, stated that the fatal shot was fired from about an inch away, which did not align with Sirhan's position. Witnesses, including journalist John Pilger, have also expressed doubt, claiming that the official explanation does not match what they saw that night.

The notion of a second gunman gained further traction due to concerns about the number of bullets fired. Sirhan's gun held eight rounds, yet witnesses claimed that as many as thirteen shots were fired. Some reported seeing bullet holes in the hotel's pantry door frames, which were later destroyed by authorities. Kennedy's son, Robert F. Kennedy Jr., has publicly questioned how so many bullets could have been fired from a gun that only held eight rounds. These details have led many to suspect that Sirhan was not the only shooter and that another gunman may have fired the fatal shots.

Further controversy emerged in 2007 when forensic audio expert Philip Van Praag analyzed a recording of the shooting captured by journalist Stanislaw Pruszynski. According to Van Praag, the tape reveals evidence of at least thirteen gunshots, with some fired so closely together that it would have been impossible for a single shooter to fire them all. He also claimed that different sound patterns suggested multiple guns were used. However, other audio experts have challenged this conclusion, arguing that the recording only captured eight gunshots. Some have dismissed Van Praag's findings, but for many, the discrepancies remain troubling.

Forensic analysis has also raised serious doubts about the case. In 1975, a judge convened a panel of seven experts to reexamine the ballistic evidence. They found that while the bullets recovered from Kennedy's body matched each other, they could not definitively be linked to Sirhan's revolver. Lead crime scene investigator DeWayne Wolfer had testified at trial that the bullet removed from Kennedy was fired from Sirhan's gun, but the forensic panel accused him of conducting a careless investigation. An internal police report later surfaced, stating that the bullet that struck Kennedy was not fired from Sirhan's weapon. In 2011, Sirhan's defense attorneys argued in court that the bullet presented as evidence in his trial had been switched, further fueling suspicions of a cover-up.

One of the most frequently discussed theories involves Thane Eugene Cesar, a security guard hired to protect Kennedy that night. Cesar, who worked at Lockheed Aircraft and held a high-level security clearance, had strong political views and was known to be staunchly anti-Kennedy. Some accounts suggest that he was in the perfect position to fire the fatal shot. He admitted to drawing his weapon during the shooting but claimed it was a .38-caliber gun, different from the .22-caliber bullets found in Kennedy. Strangely, the LAPD never considered him a suspect and did not inspect his weapon. Later, inconsistencies emerged in his statements. He initially claimed that he had sold his personal .22-caliber handgun before the assassination, but a receipt surfaced showing that he had actually sold it months after the shooting. Some researchers believe Cesar was the second gunman and that Sirhan's role was merely a distraction. Robert F. Kennedy Jr. has publicly accused Cesar of being the real killer, though Cesar denied any involvement.

Beyond the second shooter theory, some believe that Sirhan himself may have been manipulated into committing the crime. The idea that he was a "Manchurian candidate"—a brainwashed assassin acting under hypnosis—has been explored in detail. Sirhan has consistently claimed that he has no memory of the assassination. His defense team has argued that he was hypnotized and programmed to carry out the attack. In 2010, his lawyers even suggested that the CIA had used mind control techniques on him, making him an unwitting participant in a larger plot. Prison psychologist Edward Simson-Kallas reportedly supported this theory, stating that Sirhan's behavior showed signs of mind control.

Another mystery that has persisted involves a woman in a polka-dot dress. Several witnesses reported seeing her with Sirhan before and after the assassination. One campaign worker, Sandra Serrano, stated that she saw the woman with two men shortly before the shooting. After the shots were fired, she claimed the woman ran past her shouting, "We shot him! We shot Kennedy!" Other witnesses also recalled seeing a woman in a polka-dot dress in the kitchen area where the shooting took place. However, police investigators dismissed these claims, and one report suggested that Serrano had later retracted her statement under pressure. Despite this, some believe that she was coerced into changing her story. A retired LAPD officer, Paul Sharaga, also stated that an elderly couple approached him at the scene, claiming they had overheard a young couple celebrating Kennedy's death. However, his official report on the matter mysteriously disappeared, further adding to suspicions that key evidence was covered up.

The possibility of CIA involvement has also been raised. In 2006, journalist Shane O'Sullivan released a documentary suggesting that three CIA operatives were present at the Ambassador Hotel the night Kennedy was shot. He claimed that video footage from the event showed three men identified as high-ranking CIA officials. However, upon closer examination, some of these men were later identified as sales executives attending a company convention. O'Sullivan stood by his claims, arguing that the company was a known CIA front. Though the theory has not been proven, it remains one of the many unsettling aspects of the case.

Kennedy's family members have also expressed doubts about the official version of events. Robert F. Kennedy Jr. has stated that he believes his father was the victim of a conspiracy, much like his uncle, John F. Kennedy. He has criticized the Warren Commission's findings on his uncle's assassination and believes that similar forces were at play in his father's murder. While no definitive proof of a broader conspiracy has ever been uncovered, the numerous inconsistencies, missing evidence, and conflicting witness statements have kept speculation alive for decades.

The assassination of Robert F. Kennedy remains one of the most controversial moments in American history. Officially, Sirhan Sirhan acted alone, but countless questions remain unanswered. The doubts surrounding the number of shots fired, the location of Kennedy's wounds, the presence of additional suspects, and the possibility of psychological manipulation have all contributed to the belief that the truth has not been fully revealed. Despite official investigations dismissing these theories, public skepticism persists. The unresolved mysteries continue to haunt those who believe that more than one gunman was involved and that powerful forces worked to conceal the truth. Until every question is answered and all evidence is brought to light, the speculation surrounding Robert F. Kennedy's assassination will not fade.

5.3 Conspiracy Theory - Martin Luther King Jr.

Conspiracy theories have always fascinated the public, especially when they involve political assassinations. The death of Martin Luther King Jr. on April 4, 1968, in Memphis, Tennessee, remains one of the most debated events in American history. Officially, James Earl Ray was convicted as the lone assassin, but doubts have surrounded the case for decades. Theories of government involvement, the presence of other conspirators, and the idea that Ray was a scapegoat have kept the controversy alive. The assassination of King, a leader who fought tirelessly for civil rights, was a moment of profound loss for the nation. However, the circumstances surrounding his death have never been fully accepted by those who believe that a larger plot was at play.

King was assassinated on the balcony of the Lorraine Motel, just one day after delivering his famous "I've Been to the Mountaintop" speech. His murder sent shockwaves through the civil rights movement, but almost immediately, questions arose about how the crime was handled. The FBI had illegally spied on King for years, attempting to discredit him and even encouraging him to commit suicide. Many found it suspicious that the very agency that had spent years trying to destroy his reputation was now leading the investigation into his death. James Earl Ray initially confessed to the crime, but he later recanted, claiming that he had been coerced into admitting guilt. His sudden reversal led many to believe that he was forced to take the blame while the real perpetrators remained free.

In 1979, the United States House Select Committee on Assassinations (HSCA) concluded that there was likely a conspiracy in King's assassination. The committee suggested that Ray may have been acting on behalf of a larger network, though they stopped short of naming who else might have been involved. This official recognition of a possible conspiracy only deepened public doubts. In 1999, a civil trial in Memphis resulted in a jury unanimously ruling that King's assassination was the result of a conspiracy involving government agencies, organized crime, and a man named Raoul, who had allegedly set up Ray as the fall guy. Coretta Scott King, King's widow, spoke after the verdict, stating that there was overwhelming evidence of a high-level conspiracy. The jury's finding strengthened the belief that Ray had been manipulated into taking the blame while the true masterminds remained hidden.

One of the leading figures advocating for Ray's innocence was William F. Pepper, a friend of King who spent years fighting for a new trial. Pepper argued that Ray was framed and that a Special Forces hit team had been assigned to kill

King if the initial plan failed. He suggested that government forces had orchestrated the assassination and later covered up their involvement. During a televised mock trial, a jury found Ray not guilty, further fueling speculation that the official narrative was flawed. However, legal attempts to overturn Ray's conviction repeatedly failed.

Another strong voice in the conspiracy debate was Mark Lane, a lawyer and writer who had previously challenged the official account of President John F. Kennedy's assassination. Lane became Ray's attorney and argued that his client had been set up as a pawn in a much larger plot. He co-wrote a book with activist Dick Gregory, alleging that government agencies had played a role in King's assassination. Lane's influence helped keep the conspiracy theories alive, leading many to question whether Ray had truly acted alone.

The ballistics evidence in the case also raised concerns. The FBI's initial tests on the rifle allegedly used to kill King were inconclusive. Years later, further tests showed that the bullets from the murder weapon did not have distinct markings matching them to the gun. If the bullet that killed King could not be definitively linked to Ray's rifle, then how could anyone be certain that he was the gunman? This forensic uncertainty cast further doubt on the official story, with some believing that key evidence had been manipulated or even planted.

Beyond the crime scene evidence, the FBI's history of hostility toward King played a significant role in conspiracy theories. J. Edgar Hoover, the longtime director of the FBI, saw King as a threat and labeled him "the most notorious liar in the country." The FBI had wiretapped King's phones, monitored his every move, and attempted to destroy his reputation. A shocking internal memo from the FBI even suggested that King should take his own life. Many questioned whether an agency that had worked so aggressively against King could be trusted to conduct an impartial investigation into his death.

The FBI also spread false claims that King was secretly a Communist. Hoover personally told Attorney General

Robert F. Kennedy that King was involved in Communist activities, leading to the authorization of further surveillance. Some FBI documents even stated that King was a dedicated Marxist-Leninist. However, King himself dismissed such allegations, saying he was tired of hearing accusations that the civil rights movement had been infiltrated by Communists. To many, the FBI's determination to undermine King suggested that they had both the motive and the means to orchestrate his assassination.

The Memphis Police Department's actions on the day of the assassination also raised eyebrows. King had been under surveillance, and police had even assigned four officers to protect him. Yet, just before the assassination, those officers were suddenly recalled, leaving King exposed. This unexplained withdrawal of security led many to suspect that the police had knowingly allowed the assassination to take place. Additionally, two Black detectives who had been monitoring King were pulled from their posts shortly before the shooting, supposedly due to threats against their lives. The lack of police protection at the crucial moment when King was shot has been one of the most suspicious aspects of the case.

Beyond law enforcement, some have pointed to organized crime as a possible player in the assassination. Loyd Jowers, a Memphis businessman, claimed that he had been paid to help facilitate the murder. He alleged that a local mobster named Frank Liberto had offered him $100,000 to assist in the operation. Jowers even suggested that a Memphis police lieutenant, Earl Clark, had actually pulled the trigger. His claims were central to the 1999 civil trial, in which the jury found that King had been killed as part of a broad conspiracy.

The King family has consistently maintained that Ray was innocent and that the real killers were protected by powerful institutions. King's son, Dexter, personally met with Ray in prison and expressed his belief that Ray was not responsible. King's daughter, Bernice, also voiced her conviction that the assassination was the result of a well-coordinated conspiracy. Even those who had worked closely with King, such as Andrew Young and James

Lawson, expressed doubts that Ray had acted alone. The belief that a much larger force had orchestrated the assassination has persisted for decades, driven by inconsistencies in the investigation and the testimonies of those who knew King best.

While the HSCA concluded that there was likely a conspiracy, it ruled out federal agencies as being directly involved. Instead, it suggested that southern white supremacist groups may have played a role. However, many remain skeptical of this conclusion, believing that the FBI, CIA, or other government entities could have been involved in the plot or its cover-up. The idea that crucial documents may have been destroyed before the committee's investigation has only strengthened the belief that the full truth has never been revealed.

Even though a civil jury found that King's death was the result of a conspiracy, the U.S. Department of Justice later reexamined the case and found no credible evidence to support this conclusion. They dismissed Jowers' statements as unreliable and argued that there was no solid proof linking the mafia or government agencies to the crime. Despite this official position, skepticism remains widespread. Many believe that the government had a strong interest in silencing King, who had become increasingly vocal about issues beyond civil rights, including poverty and the Vietnam War.

For some, the assassination of Martin Luther King Jr. was not just the murder of a civil rights leader but the silencing of a revolutionary voice. He was challenging the entire structure of American society, advocating for economic justice and an end to war. His growing influence made him a target, and those who wanted to maintain the status quo had every reason to stop him. Whether through direct action or by allowing the assassination to happen, many believe that the forces of power ensured that King would not live to see his dream realized.

Decades later, the full truth behind King's assassination remains elusive. The case is filled with contradictions, missing evidence, and conflicting testimonies. While some accept the official explanation, others remain convinced that the assassination was a carefully orchestrated event, with Ray serving as a convenient scapegoat. The debate over King's death is not just about history—it is about the ongoing struggle for justice and accountability. Until every unanswered question is resolved, the suspicions surrounding his assassination will persist, reminding the world that even in the pursuit of truth, obstacles remain.

Chapter 6: The Role of Government Secrecy and Declassified Records

For as long as governments have existed, secrecy has played a powerful role in shaping history. Some information is kept hidden to protect national security, while other details remain classified to prevent panic or to shield political figures from controversy. But as time passes, secrecy often clashes with the public's right to know. This is where declassified records come in—offering a chance to uncover long-buried truths, correct misunderstandings, and allow history to be seen in its fullest light.

One of the most well-known examples of government secrecy is the assassination of President John F. Kennedy (JFK) in 1963. Almost immediately after his death, questions arose about what really happened in Dealey Plaza, Dallas. The Warren Commission, set up by President

Lyndon B. Johnson, concluded that Lee Harvey Oswald acted alone in killing Kennedy. But not everyone accepted this explanation. Over the decades, thousands of files related to the assassination were kept classified, fueling speculation that the full story had not been told.

The JFK Records Act of 1992 was a significant step toward government transparency. This law required all remaining classified records related to Kennedy's assassination to be reviewed and released to the public. Some files have been declassified, but even today, certain documents remain sealed. This raises an important question: if a government truly serves its people, should it have the right to withhold historical information indefinitely?

Government secrecy isn't just about assassinations. It extends into many areas, including military operations, covert intelligence programs, and diplomatic affairs. During the Cold War, for example, both the United States and the Soviet Union conducted secret activities that only came to light years later. The CIA's involvement in coups, espionage missions, and even mind-control experiments like MKUltra were hidden from the public for decades. When such details were finally revealed, they changed how people viewed their government and its actions.

Declassified records play a crucial role in correcting the historical record. Without them, many major events would remain misunderstood or entirely hidden. Consider the Pentagon Papers, which were leaked in the 1970s and revealed that the U.S. government had misled the public about the Vietnam War. These documents showed that officials knew the war was unwinnable but continued to escalate it anyway. Had these records remained secret, the American people might never have known the full extent of their government's actions.

Another major event involving secrecy was the Watergate scandal, which led to President Richard Nixon's resignation in 1974. Government officials tried to cover up illegal activities, but declassified records and investigative journalism exposed the truth. The scandal proved that secrecy can be dangerous when used to hide corruption rather than protect national security.

In more recent history, the 9/11 attacks in 2001 led to new debates over secrecy and transparency. The government classified many details related to the attack and its aftermath, including portions of the 9/11 Commission Report. Some of these documents were eventually declassified, revealing insights about foreign involvement and intelligence failures. However, many Americans still believe that key details remain hidden, reinforcing the idea that government secrecy sometimes breeds distrust.

One of the most controversial moments in declassification history came in 2017, when President Donald Trump announced the release of thousands of JFK assassination records. This decision was seen as a major step toward uncovering long-held secrets. However, some files were still withheld, leading to frustration among historians and researchers. The question remained: if these documents had been kept secret for more than 50 years, what was still too sensitive to reveal?

Declassified records also serve as evidence for justice. In the case of Dr. Martin Luther King Jr.'s assassination in 1968, government files have provided insight into the FBI's surveillance of King. Documents released in later years showed that J. Edgar Hoover's FBI considered King a threat and monitored him extensively. While this does not prove direct involvement in his assassination, it raises ethical concerns about how intelligence agencies can be used to target political figures.

Similarly, declassified records have revealed new details about the assassination of Senator Robert F. Kennedy (RFK). While Sirhan Sirhan was convicted of the crime, some records suggest that other individuals were present at the scene, leading to renewed calls for a deeper investigation. These cases highlight how declassification isn't just about history—it's about justice, accountability, and ensuring that the truth is fully known.

But while declassification is essential, it also comes with challenges. Some information, if revealed too soon, could endanger national security or international relations. This is why governments often use redactions, blacking out certain parts of documents before releasing them to the public. However, when too much is redacted, it can create even more suspicion, as people wonder what is being hidden.

Secrecy can also be used as a tool for political power. Governments sometimes classify records not to protect the nation, but to protect individuals in power. This is why whistleblowers—people who expose hidden government actions—have played a crucial role in history. Figures like Daniel Ellsberg (Pentagon Papers), Edward Snowden (NSA surveillance), and Julian Assange (WikiLeaks) have all revealed classified information that sparked worldwide debates. Their actions raise ethical questions: when does government secrecy cross the line into deception?

The fight between secrecy and transparency continues in the digital age. With the rise of the internet, classified information can be leaked faster than ever before. Governments are now struggling to control the flow of information while balancing the public's right to know. The challenge is ensuring that secrecy is used for legitimate security reasons rather than as a way to hide uncomfortable truths.

Looking ahead, the role of declassified records will only grow in importance. As more files from the JFK, RFK, and MLK assassinations are released, the public may finally get a clearer picture of events that shaped American history. Similarly, as records from recent wars, intelligence operations, and political scandals become available, they will help future generations understand the past with greater accuracy.

Chapter 7: Lessons from History and Their Relevance Today

History is more than just a record of past events—it is a guide that helps us understand the present and shape the future. Some of the most defining moments in American history come from the assassinations of President John F. Kennedy (JFK), Senator Robert F. Kennedy (RFK), and Dr. Martin Luther King Jr. (MLK). These three leaders were not only symbols of hope and progress but also figures whose deaths left behind deep scars and lingering questions. Their assassinations forced the country to confront government secrecy, political violence, and the limits of democracy. The lessons drawn from these tragedies remain as relevant today as they were decades ago.

One of the most powerful lessons from these events is the danger of secrecy in government affairs. In each of these assassinations, key records were withheld, intelligence agencies operated in the shadows, and crucial details remained classified for decades. When JFK was shot in Dallas on November 22, 1963, the government launched an investigation, but the Warren Commission's findings left more questions than answers. It concluded that Lee Harvey Oswald acted alone, but many Americans remained skeptical. The secrecy surrounding the investigation fueled mistrust, leading to speculation that the full truth had not been told. When governments choose secrecy over transparency, public confidence is eroded—a lesson that remains relevant today.

The same pattern emerged after the assassinations of RFK and MLK in 1968. RFK was killed while campaigning in Los Angeles, and MLK was assassinated in Memphis just months earlier. In both cases, official investigations faced criticism for ignoring key evidence, dismissing alternative suspects, and failing to address concerns raised by the victims' families. The House Select Committee on Assassinations (HSCA), formed in the 1970s, later challenged some of the original findings, suggesting that there was a high probability that JFK's assassination involved more than one shooter and that MLK's murder may have been the result of a conspiracy. These findings underscored a crucial lesson—when investigations lack thoroughness and transparency, history becomes clouded, and justice is left incomplete.

Another major lesson from these assassinations is that political violence threatens democracy. JFK, RFK, and MLK represented change, reform, and a vision for a better America. Their deaths altered the course of history, leaving behind a sense of unfinished work. JFK had championed civil rights, space exploration, and diplomacy, RFK was poised to challenge corruption and end the Vietnam War, and MLK was leading the Poor People's Campaign to fight economic inequality. Their assassinations were not just personal tragedies—they were national turning points that reshaped the country's future. Today, as political tensions rise and violence remains a threat, history warns us that when leaders are silenced, democracy itself is at risk.

The investigations into these assassinations also reveal the importance of independent oversight and public accountability. The original Warren Commission findings on JFK's murder were widely accepted at first, but as classified documents were gradually released, inconsistencies emerged. Had the government committed to full transparency from the beginning, decades of speculation and distrust might have been avoided. Similarly, the initial investigation into MLK's assassination pointed to James Earl Ray as the sole shooter, yet MLK's own family and many historians disputed this version of events, arguing that the case deserved deeper scrutiny. These cases remind us that history demands accountability, and when official investigations fail to provide clear answers, the public will keep asking questions.

Moreover, these assassinations reshaped laws and government policies. The backlash against the secrecy surrounding JFK's murder led to the JFK Records Act of 1992, which required the release of all assassination-related documents. This law was a direct response to public pressure for transparency, proving that citizens have the power to demand the truth from their government. Likewise, after MLK's death, the nation saw the passage of civil rights protections, but the fight for racial and economic justice remains ongoing. These moments in history show that when people unite to demand answers, they can force change, even in the face of government resistance.

In today's world, the lessons from these assassinations remain deeply relevant. The balance between national security and the right to know, the role of government agencies in shaping historical narratives, and the dangers of political violence are issues that continue to shape America. History warns us that when truth is withheld, speculation fills the void, and when justice is delayed, wounds remain open. Understanding these events helps ensure that future generations learn from the past rather than repeat its mistakes.

7.1 The Importance of Understanding American History

History is often seen as something that belongs in textbooks or museums, but in reality, it is a living force that continues to shape the world today. The assassinations of JFK, RFK, and MLK are not just historical moments; they are lessons in truth, justice, and accountability. Understanding these events is essential to understanding America itself.

One of the biggest reasons to study history is to prevent misinformation and protect facts from distortion. Over the years, the secrecy surrounding these assassinations has allowed countless theories, speculation, and misinformation to thrive. When facts are buried, the truth becomes harder to separate from fiction. By studying primary sources, declassified records, and credible investigations, we can ensure that history is based on evidence, not speculation.

Another reason why learning about these events matters is that they teach us about the struggle for justice. MLK's assassination was not just the loss of a leader—it was a defining moment in the civil rights movement. His death forced the country to confront the reality of racial injustice, leading to renewed efforts for equality. Similarly, RFK's murder cut short a campaign that could have transformed America's political landscape. By understanding these figures and their work, we gain insight into the ongoing fight for justice today.

Understanding history also makes us better citizens. When people learn about events like the JFK Records Act, they realize that public pressure can lead to change. When they see how past investigations were mishandled, they become more aware of the need for government accountability. This awareness translates into voting, activism, and civic engagement, ensuring that leaders are held responsible for their actions.

Moreover, studying these assassinations reveals the dangers of unchecked government power. The FBI's surveillance of

MLK, the secrecy surrounding JFK's murder, and the questions left unanswered about RFK's death show how easily power can be abused or misused. History teaches us to question authority, demand transparency, and fight for the truth, no matter how long it takes.

In the end, history is not just about remembering the past—it is about shaping the future. The deaths of JFK, RFK, and MLK were turning points that forced the nation to reflect on its values, laws, and responsibilities. By studying these events, we gain the tools to protect democracy, promote justice, and ensure that the mistakes of the past are never repeated.

The lessons from these assassinations remain profoundly relevant today. They teach us that government secrecy must always be challenged, political violence must never be normalized, and the pursuit of truth must never be abandoned. Understanding history is not optional—it is a responsibility. Only by looking back can we move forward, ensuring that the ideals these leaders fought for continue to guide us toward a better, more just America.

CONCLUSION

The assassinations of JFK, RFK, and MLK marked one of the darkest periods in American history. These were trying times, filled with political unrest, racial tensions, and a growing distrust in the government. Each of these men represented hope, change, and a vision for a better America, yet they were gunned down in cold blood before their work could be completed. Their deaths left a nation in mourning and a world searching for answers.

Over the decades, multiple presidents have attempted to uncover the full truth, from Lyndon B. Johnson's Warren Commission to Jimmy Carter's congressional reinvestigation, and later, George H.W. Bush's push for declassification. In 2017, Donald Trump ordered the release of thousands of government documents, and now, he is once again reopening the discussion on what remains hidden. The decision to review these cases is not just about history—it is about justice, accountability, and restoring trust in government institutions.

For America, and for the world, these investigations matter. They are a reminder that the truth cannot stay buried forever. The demand for transparency is not just about the past—it is about ensuring that democracy remains strong, that power is held accountable, and that the voices of those who fought for justice are never silenced. Now, as the country awaits the full release of these records, one question remains: Will this finally bring the answers that history has long denied us?

Made in United States
Troutdale, OR
03/21/2025